M000015132

DISCOVERING
HOPE

Stuart Parkin

Grosvenor House
Publishing Limited

All rights reserved
Copyright © Stuart Parkin, 2020

The right of Stuart Parkin to be identified as the author of this
work has been asserted in accordance with Section 78
of the Copyright, Designs and Patents Act 1988

The book cover is copyright to Stuart Parkin

This book is published by
Grosvenor House Publishing Ltd
Link House
140 The Broadway, Tolworth, Surrey, KT6 7HT.
www.grosvenorhousepublishing.co.uk

This book is sold subject to the conditions that it shall not, by way of
trade or otherwise, be lent, resold, hired out or otherwise circulated
without the author's or publisher's prior consent in any form of binding or
cover other than that in which it is published and
without a similar condition including this condition being imposed
on the subsequent purchaser.

A CIP record for this book
is available from the British Library

ISBN 978-1-83975-397-8

When things in our lives do not go as we would like, we can become frustrated. If the situation persists over a sustained period, such as a year with a pandemic, we can lose hope, defined as 'a desire for a particular thing to happen'. This small book is designed to maximize your hopefulness, providing a variety of things you can do to help you on your journey.

Turn to any page of this book and you will be a step towards what you wish to be.

"Hope is being able to see the light despite all the darkness." *Desmund Tutu*

"Hope is passion for what is possible."
Soren Kierkegaard

"Once you choose hope, anything is possible,"
Christopher Reeve

"Dwell in possibility," *Emily Dickinson*

"Learn from yesterday, live for today, hope for tomorrow," *Albert Einstein*

"Hope and fear cannot occupy the same space. Invite one to stay," *Maya Angelou*

"To live without hope is to cease to live,"
Fyodor Dostoevsky

"The sky is not the limit, your mind is,"
Marilyn Monroe

Love

Be in love and you will be hopeful for those you
love if not for yourself.

"The salvation of man is through love and is love."
Viktor Frankel

Action Stations

Very often, action – even if the wrong action –
feels much better than doing nothing. Act!

"Buy the ticket, take the ride." *Hunter S. Thompson*

Freshly Cut Grass

The smell of freshly cut grass always makes me breathe deeply and feel so good. Which smells make you feel instantly relaxed? Make a note what they are, and if you can, bottle them!

"No man is a failure who is enjoying life."
William Feather

Anxiety

When you are anxious, things are typically out of control. Take time out and focus on something over which you have complete control, such as making a cup of tea for someone.

"You are not a drop in the ocean, you are the entire ocean in a drop." *Rumi*

Body Therapy

Lightly run the tips of your fingers across the palms of your hands and see how relaxing that is. Body therapies help, as your nerves are physically soothed, invigorating the body and soul.

"Without deviation from the norm progress is not possible." *Frank Zappa*

Taking Control

When everything seems out of our control, what can or should you do? Take control! Take control of things you *can* control: your breath; what you choose to hear, to eat, to drink, to touch, to feel. Take control, one sense at a time, and feel your strength return.

"Either you run the day, or the day runs you."
Jim Rohn

Gratitude

When we are focused on what we have, we are a safe
distance from hopelessness.

"Joy is the simplest form of gratitude." *Karl Barth*

Indulge

Chemicals in the body help to enhance our mood and outlook. Exercise, music, essential oils, laughter, ginseng, chocolate, and spicy foods, can all boost these chemicals and our feel-good factor. Be kind to yourself. Indulge.

"Life is the dancer and you are the dance."
Eckhart Tolle

Children

Be more like your children, attend to your inner child, pretend at least to take every moment as it comes and enjoy the small pleasures of life. If this is difficult, for the next seconds pretend to walk around the room like a robot!

"Nothing ever becomes real until experienced."
John Keats

Empathy

Understanding how others feel is the key to connection.
While we retain the ability to connect with others
and to think beyond our own experience, we
will always have hope.

"Be kind, for everyone you meet is fighting a
harder battle." *Plato*

Empowerment

Hopelessness excels when you no longer feel you are in control of your life. Start writing a small diary today, and this will be the first step to understanding your thoughts and exactly what you are feeling.

"A smooth sea never made a skillful mariner."
(English proverb)

Garden

Gardeners are some of the most positive and relaxed of people. They set their own agenda, whilst understanding and accepting that some things are way beyond them – classically, the weather!

"Keep your face to the sun and you will never see the shadows." *Helen Keller*

Inhibitions

Being strong mentally is as much to do with our ability to relax/let go of our inhibitions. Swim naked in the ocean at dusk. Sing in the park.

"Life is ten percent what happens to you and ninety percent how you respond to it." *Lou Holtz*

Causes to Hope

Find examples of apparent lost causes which have been miraculously resolved. These, if nothing else, will be reminders why we should always hope.

"A champion is someone who gets up when he cannot." *Jack Dempsey*

Choice

You can see everything as a threat, or everything as an opportunity. You can decide that everyone is out to get you, or that everyone is basically decent and will try to help you. It's your choice.

"Whether you think you can or think you can't, you're right." *Henry Ford*

Learning

Formal or informal discovery is one of the most powerful and empowering things. When you acquire knowledge, you feel strength returning to your body and mind. Learn this!

"To plant a garden is to believe in tomorrow."
Audrey Hepburn

Focus

When you are focused on what you will do, you are not making assessments – good or bad – about the state of the world, your own or other people's lives. You are simply focused. Find something that absorbs you.

"Always remember that your focus determines your reality." *George Lucas*

Music

To relax, to energize, to soothe... make music a key
feature of your life.

"If music be the food of life, play on."
William Shakespeare

Family

Family reminds us of love, loyalty, and unconditional bonds, and is a bedrock of reliability and support. These things in our lives remind us what matters and what does not. Have a picture of your loved ones close at hand.

"The journey is where we find perspective."
Alison Levine

Trickery

When you genuinely laugh, your body releases chemicals called endorphins, which make you feel good. Science has revealed that the same endorphins are released when you *pretend* to laugh. Try it, and see how you feel.

"The difference between insanity and genius is measured only by success." *Bruce Feirstein*

Acupressure

The reason why having your hair washed is so relaxing
is because all the acupressure points on your head
are being massaged. Massaging your scalp is not
only relaxing, but also promotes blood flow and
a positive sensation.

"Little minds are tamed and subdued by misfortune,
but great minds rise above them." *Washington Irving*

Respite

'Hitting the wall' is a term used in marathon running, when all energy and hope are lost. The way to avoid this state is to pace yourself and conserve your energy, effort, and thinking, from the start of the challenge.

"Love the life you live. Live the life you love."
Bob Marley

Sharing

Sharing with others is a great thing to do, but do not just share the good things! Sharing your problems/ negative emotions is key to unloading the burden you feel. It is also a step away from being alone, and a step towards solving your problems.

"Your biggest opportunity may be where you are now."
Napoleon Hill

Attitude

Circumstances will test us, but how we react is up to us. Being angry or sad, frustrated, or galvanized. On an issue that does not matter, practice being happy and sad, irritated and not. Experience how you get to decide what your reaction is.

"Believe you can, and you are halfway there."
Theodore Roosevelt

Joy

A moment of bliss or being carefree. A funny comic skit that makes you laugh uncontrollably, a puppy video, swimming happily in the ocean. Whatever delivers 'carefree', reminds you how you can be.

"Enthusiasm is the mother of effort, and without it nothing great was ever achieved."
Ralph Waldo Emerson

People

People the world over have much more in common
than not, are well intentioned, and have common
cause. Know this, so that you can be hopeful about
the future.

"When the world says, 'Give up,' Hope whispers,
'Try it one more time.'" *Anon*

Now

If you can focus on the moment, you will not only be more present in the conversation you are having, but you will also be better able to communicate and connect. Avoid distractions which hold you back.

"Everyone is born a genius, but the process of living de-geniuses them." *Buckminster Fuller*

Simplify

Do fewer things, but make them things that matter.
Have fewer things, but make them things you treasure.
Less is more.

"We cannot change the cards we are dealt, just how
we play them." *Randy Pausch*

Celebrate

Learn to celebrate successes – yours, your family's, and friends', and those of others. These positive moments of recognition help fortify you for the challenges ahead.

"The grateful heart will always find opportunities to express its gratitude." *Aesop*

Nostalgia

Live richly today, as these memories will be powerful tomorrow. Reflect on great adventures, laughter, moments of pride and joy, and you will be emboldened to create more today and tomorrow.

"Do not count the days, make the days count."
Muhammad Ali

Yoga

Better stretching and breathing gained from practicing yoga lead to better circulation and a calmer mind. Breathe as you hope to be: steady, resilient, and optimistic. Hear your breath. Repeat.

"Somewhere something incredible is waiting to be known." *Carl Sagan*

Subconscious

Post uplifting notes around your home. Before too long you will not even notice them, but your subconscious mind will be fed a steady stream of positivity.

"Quality is never an accident." *John Ruskin*

Perspective

If you face a challenge that seems insurmountable,
think of something truly insurmountable. Yes, get it
into perspective. There are very few things that we truly
cannot overcome with focus and patience.

"Where there is no hope it is incumbent on us
to invent it." *Albert Camus*

Proactive

When you are proactive, whilst the blood flows in your arteries, as you act – whatever the outlook – all outcomes remain possible. Stop, and the conclusion is inevitable.

"It always seems impossible until it is done."
Nelson Mandela

Balance

The secret to a truly sustainable, guilt-free, positive outlook, is to occasionally splurge. But to function effectively, your habits should ensure a steady diet of fresh air, water, exercise, and diet. Steady as she goes should be your mantra.

"Whatever you are, be a good one." *Abraham Lincoln*

Opportunity

No-one likes to be trapped. By providing yourself with some options, you not only free yourself from real constraints, but in doing so you also change your mindset.

"You are braver than you believe, smarter than you seem, and stronger than you think."
A.A. Milne/Winnie the Pooh

Community

Knowing we are all in this together, that we are not alone, that others care about the things we care about, provides comfort but also knowledge to manage and then overcome issues.

"Never doubt that a small group of thoughtful, committed citizens can change the world; indeed, it's the only thing that ever has." *Margaret Mead*

Safety Switch

When you are feeling really stressed, stop what you are doing, turn off the lights, shut your eyes, and breathe deeply – a human form of reboot. Sitting down, thrust both of your arms up to make a star shape. Repeat this for thirty seconds and see how you feel.

"Some of us think that holding on makes us strong, but sometimes it is better to let go." *Herman Hesse*

Money

Money certainly makes life easier, but lack of it can make for genuine frustration and difficulty. So, make what you value most things that have nothing to do with money, and better still, things that are in abundance. For example, a hearty laugh, the morning sunrise, the first coffee of the day.

"I would rather be able to appreciate things I cannot have than to have things I cannot appreciate."
Elbert Hubbard

Addiction

When we are addicted to anything, we are out of
control. So, choose addictions that help you realize
your dreams. Start by being addicted to being positive
about how you will spend your day.

"Good decision comes from experience. Experience
comes from making bad decisions." *Mark Twain*

Habit Breaking

If you routinely think negatively, change your routine.
Walk away from your desk; go outside; sit in the park;
have a cat nap; mix things up.

"You are never a loser until you quit trying."
Mike Ditka

Dialing Down

There are things that wind you up, that dial up tension in your life. Consciously plan to limit, if not remove, these things one by one. Do this, and if nothing else, you will feel less stressed.

"What we see depends mainly on what we look for."
Sir John Lubbock

Time Heals All

Hope stems from understanding that in time, all that we are unhappy about will be resolved. Either our thinking will change, or circumstances will. Either way, life will go on.

"All things change, nothing perishes." *Ovid*

Collaboration

Many hands (and minds) make for lighter work.
When we can see no path forward, we can feel
confused or lost. Where you can, talk about
it/share your challenge with others.

"Where there is ruin, there is hope for treasure." *Rumi*

Make Love

In the moment and beyond it, making love leads to a euphoric state, benefiting mind and body, as it achieves physical and mental connectedness.

'One's destination is never a place, but a new way of seeing things.' *Henry Miller*.

Reasoning

If you can accept that everything happens for a reason,
then you are closer to knowing that all things
ultimately work out for the best!

"Our aspirations are our possibilities." *Samuel Johnson*

Silver Linings

Very often, even when stories end badly, there are also silver linings. Similarly, when your outlook seems grim, it is not usually all bad; it is more a question of where you wish to focus. Practice focusing on the silver linings and you will always be hopeful.

"While there is life there is hope." *Cicero*

Treatment

A hot towel on your face, a bubble bath, a great stretch after sitting down. Comforting treatments bring peace to body and mind. Treat yourself.

"Dream as if you will live forever; live as if you will die today." *James Dean*

Tomorrow

The present moment is somehow less difficult when we are told that we will have a second chance, or that 'tomorrow is a new day'. The idea of starting afresh boosts our mind and spirit. Do not wait for tomorrow: restart now!

"Tomorrow belongs to those who hear it coming."
David Bowie, 'Heroes'

Touch

To touch or be touched, to hug – a surefire way
to raise the spirits.

"Do or do not. There is no try." *Yoda*,
'The Empire Strikes Back'

Avoid Being Overstretched

Even the most optimistic person can, under the right circumstances, lose hope. A combination of too much pressure, too few resources (time/money), and little support (family/friends/colleagues), can dull our outlook. A healthy challenge is not the same as being stretched in all respects.

"Do not let what you can't do interfere with what you can do." *John R Wooden*

Language

"I hope so", "I'm hopeful", and "I'm hoping",
are better words to practice than "It's hopeless",
"I can't", and "It won't". But "I can" and
"I will" are even better.

"As you think, so you shall become." *Bruce Lee*

Redefine

A problem is a problem until you redefine it. Break it down, look at similarities to past challenges, and get others to help you with it. You get to decide how great a problem is, and how and when you will confront it.

"Living well does not mean avoiding suffering but suffering for the right reasons." *Mark Manson*

Beauty

There is so much beauty surrounding all of us. Focus on the delicacy of the petals of a flower, or the light shining through your child's hair. Wherever you find beauty, it will enhance your state of mind.

"People who are unable to motivate themselves must be content with mediocrity, no matter how impressive their other talents." *Andrew Carnegie*

Order/Organisation

Confusion, and worse still chaos, causes negative feelings. Approach your challenges with a system or some structure, and extend this to an ordered physical environment. Try it and see how much clearer and more positive your thinking becomes.

"I have noticed that even people who believe that everything is predestined, look before crossing the road." *Stephen Hawking*

Media Consumption

Just like the air you breathe, the media you consume day in, day out will impact your outlook. Aim to pursue positive media. Is there a 'good news' channel?

"You are only given a little spark of madness. You must not lose it." *Robin Williams*

Giving

A safe place to be. When you give to others, they benefit, but the real beneficiary is you.

"The only wealth you will keep forever is the wealth you have given away." *Marcus Aurelius*

Change

Many hope for things to stay the same. Practice eating new foods, learning new things, and being in new situations. Do this, and you will see change not as a threat to you, but as an opportunity for improvement.

"Don't get too comfortable with who you are at any given time – you may miss the opportunity to become who you want to be." *Jon Bon Jovi*

Stress

If you cannot escape the clutches of stress, weaken its hold on you. Get a massage, meditate, exercise, do whatever it takes to give body and mind a break. Step away from what stops your progress, and a step closer to feeling hopeful for what might be.

"Any person capable of angering you becomes your master." *Epictetus*

On the Clock

We all live by the diary/calendar and this is stressful,
perhaps because of how much we/others cram on to it.
We all need time, not simply to do but also to think!
Make a point of blocking out time for you to think/do
what you need to do to relax.

"It does not really matter where you are coming from,
it's where you are going that matters." *Brian Tracy*

Wander

Be a star-gazer. Watch a herd of 100,000 wildebeest migrate. See the Northern Lights change color and swirl. Look at a jumbo jet fly over, and allow yourself to be amazed that something so heavy stays airborne. When you experience wonder, all things seem possible.

"Never confuse motion with action."
Benjamin Franklin

Natural Light

SAD (or Seasonal Affective Disorder) negatively impacts the mindsets of many, and is caused by a lack of sunlight. Either get some sun or eat leafy vegetables, eggs, or salmon!

"Success is getting what you want. Happiness is wanting what you get." *Dale Carnegie*

The Best

Develop a habit of looking for the best in people and situations – or at least, the best before you see anything else! This will increase your capacity to hope.

'Stay close to anything that makes you feel glad to be alive.' *Hafez*

Release

Go to a quiet place and shout as loud as you can.
You will feel a release.

"At first dreams seem impossible, then improbable,
then inevitable." *Christopher Reeve*

Simple Pleasures

The light of the sunset, your team scoring a goal,
seeing the seed of the plant emerge. Focus on
things that build your spirits.

"To learn is to be young, however old." *Aeschylus*

Breathing

A deeply relaxed person breathes significantly less than someone that is hyperventilating. If you can breathe slightly more slowly, you will enhance your health, mentality, and outlook.

"It is not what we take up, but what we give up that makes us rich." *Henry Ward Beecher*

Nietzsche

Nietsch, the German philosopher, famously believed that the formula for happiness was, in his words, '*amar fati*' – or 'don't hope'! Accept all things the way they are, and in so doing, take the pressure off yourself. Then strive to achieve your goals.

"Every day is a fresh start. Don't measure yourself by yesterday." *Danny S Barrios*

Surrender

Surrender, not to the inevitable, not to an apparently lost cause or bad outlook, but to the realm of possibility and to the belief that in the end, by your consistent effort, things will work out for the best. The only time you fail to succeed is when you choose to stop trying.

"Every believer I have met says, 'My life turned around when I began to believe in me.'" *Robert Schiller*

Box Your Worries

Those best able to manage or avoid real stress can confront challenges and easily forget them/put them away in a mental box. Write down your concerns and imagine putting them in a metal box, then seeing yourself locking it. Better still, physically do this.

"The ultimate measure of a person is not where they stand in moments of comfort and convenience but where they stand at times of challenge and controversy." *Martin Luther King*

Challenges

Try to see a challenge as an opportunity, not a problem. See what appears at first sight to be troublesome as not all bad; view something awful as merely temporary. Practice seeing the silver lining and this will make you resilient.

"No problem can be solved from the same level of consciousness that created it." *Albert Einstein*

Heroic Action

Help an old lady across the road. Buy a round of drinks at a bar. Anonymously send some toys to an orphanage. See how you feel after doing such things.

"Those that are the happiest are those that do the most for others." *Booker T Washington*

Crisis of Hope

When we overindulge an emotion, we can easily obsess about it and, in so doing, become frustrated then angry and despondent. When you feel a strong emotion, breathe, and make a point not to react for five minutes.

"Some people feel the rain. Others just get wet."
Bob Dylan

Time Out

Tell yourself today that you will not allow anything less than positive thoughts. Today is a day when any negative idea is immediately thrown in the waste bin. Have a family member or friend help you with this.

'You'll never find a rainbow if you're looking down.'
Charlie Chaplain

Adventure

There is nothing that galvanizes the spirit more than real-life adventure. Organize a trip somewhere, doing something you have never done. Do not delay, ink out the dates in your dairy/calendar. See how simply organizing this invigorates you.

"Being realistic is the most commonly traveled road to mediocrity." *Will Smith*

Pets

Sharing your time with a pet, with its unconditional enthusiasm, wagging tail, or appreciative purr, will only make you think positively.

"What counts is not necessarily the size of the dog in the fight but the size of the fight in the dog."
Dwight D Eisenhower

Agenda

How you spend your day, your time, plays a huge part in dictating your mood. When we struggle most, the agenda of our day is usually set by others. When you can, set your own agenda.

"Build your own dreams or someone else will hire you to build theirs." *Farrah Grey*

Peer Pressure

Support of others buoys us; equally, societal or peer pressure – both of which are constant – can douse our spirits. Consciously decide where you will allow others to influence you. Set meaningful goals, and these will help you do this.

"Set your course by the stars, not the lights of very passing ship." *Omar Bradley*

Dreams

Our dreams are the window to what is possible and what we hope for. While we dream, all things are possible and we are truly alive. Ensure you get a good night's sleep.

"Logic will get you from A to B. Imagination will get you everywhere." *Albert Einstein*

Ignore the Uncontrollable–

Every day we face many challenges, some which we can impact and resolve, and others over which we have no control. Understand what they are and where to focus your energy. This will take you a step closer to a positive state.

"Worrying is like paying a debt you don't owe."
Mark Twain

Legacy

If you were on your deathbed, would you be happy to have spent so much time and energy stressing about this current issue? Most things we stress about are not worth the time. Focus your energy on those you love.

"Be soft. Do not let the world make you hard. Do not let pain make you hate. Do not let bitterness steal your sweetness." *Kurt Vonnegut*

The Past

The past is gone and what was said and done cannot be changed, but today and from now onwards, all new things are possible. Embrace this new opportunity.

"Your life requires your mindful presence in order to live it. Be here now." *Akiroq Brost*

Focus

The 'Tetris' effect instructs that where we consistently focus our attention is how we see the world. So, practice seeing positive things.

"If you are depressed, you are living in the past. If you're anxious, you're living in the future. If you're at peace, you're living in the present." *Lao Tzu*

Biorhythms

Some believe that our energy levels and outlook are determined by the calendar. They believe we function better on certain days than others. Some days you will be energized, and some pessimistic. For sure, we all have certain times of the day when we know we function better. Know when you are at your most energized/optimistic best.

"Only put off until tomorrow what you are willing to die having left undone." *Pablo Picasso*

Oxytocin

Amongst other things, oxytocin – a hormone in our body – plays an important part in reducing stress. A good hug will produce oxytocin, as will having a chat with a friend. Get social!

"Don' go through life. Grow through life."
Eric Butterworth

Meditate

Negativity hails from, amongst other areas, frustration, guilt, and powerlessness. A more positive state of mind can be found through meditation, where your focus becomes your breathing or some other singular sound or thought. If nothing else, the mental break from negativity might not transform you, but it will move you closer to being positive.

"Never give up on something you can't go a day without thinking about." *Winston Churchill*

Comedy

Laughter is an enormously powerful distraction from negative emotion, but more than that, it physically makes us feel good. Turn on the sitcom, go and see some live comedy, or hang out with someone that's funny.

"If a book of failures doesn't sell, is it a success?"
Jerry Seinfeld

Permission

We talk ourselves into situations and ways of thinking. Make a choice that for one hour a day, you will feel positive. Pick a cause or a subject that makes it easy for you to be positive – your child, reminiscing about a celebration, or a favorite event.

"When everything seems to be going against you, always remember that the airplane takes off against and not with the wind." *Henry Ford*

State of Mind

A beautiful garden needs to be nurtured with sunshine, water, and nutrients. Similarly, a 'can-do' outlook stems from a mind nurtured and nourished with a steady diet of positive thoughts, actions, and food.

"Some people grumble because the roses have thorns; I am thankful that thorns have roses." *Alphonse Karr*

Pretend

Pretend to be hopeful. Look at videos of people being positive: how do they look, sound, and come across? Remind yourself how a hopeful person is and acts. Understand this, and act as if you are hopeful, then see how it feels.

"I have missed 9000 shots in my career. I have lost almost 300 games. I have failed over and over in my life. This is why I succeed." *Michael Jordan*

Philosopher

Having a philosopher friend is a handy thing to have.
They might not always be able to solve your problems,
but they will be able to put them in context and make
them a step less problematic.

"No man ever steps in the same river twice, for it's not
the same river and he is not the same man." *Heraclitus*

Dawn

Yogis, meditators, and many that place great stock in mental clarity and peace, get up before dawn to experience the sunrise. Try it, if not for the peace, for the spectacle of the light and birth of the day.

"If you want to find happiness, find gratitude."
Steve Maraboli

Faith

Those that have 'complete faith' do not need hope, as they have total belief that all things are as they are meant to be and will work out for the best.

"Let your hopes not your hurts shape your future."
Robert H Schuller

Standards

If you must choose to live to impossible standards set by others, it is easy to lose hope. So, decide today to set your own goals, or at least ones in which you have played a part in setting.

"Always seek out the seed of triumph in any adversity." *Og Mandino*

Play

When we play or are playful, we are in a genuinely happy space. Play more.

"You can learn more about a person in an hour of play than in a year of conversation." *Plato*

Purpose

Your work and your goals are important, but remind yourself why and what you are working for? Do things on and with purpose, and you will have all the meaning in the world to remain in a positive state.

"The future belongs to those who prepare for it."
Emerson

Forgiveness

Much of our outlook for the future is based on experience of the past. When that experience has been negative, we often blame this on others and hold anger, resentment, frustration, and other emotions that drain the spirt. You do not have to forget but you need to forgive others. Do this and you will be the main beneficiary, as you boost your mindset and outlook.

"Real generosity is doing something nice for someone who will never find out." *Albert Camus*

Friendships

When you have doubts, make a point of tapping into some long-standing relationships. These will be sturdy pillars in your life experience. Like anything that is solid, these friendships will have seen good and bad times yet prevailed, and this will remind you that doubts come and go but what lasts are things that matter.

"I'm not a product of my circumstances, I'm a product of my decisions." *Steven Covey*